EMERGENCY PREPAREDNESS

LOGBOOK

Checklists, Tips, and Strategies
for Peace of Mind

Peter Pauper Press, Inc.
WHITE PLAINS, NEW YORK

PETER PAUPER PRESS
Fine Books and Gifts Since 1928

Our Company

In 1928, at the age of twenty-two, Peter Beilenson began printing books on a small press in the basement of his parents' home in Larchmont, New York. Peter—and later, his wife, Edna—sought to create fine books that sold at "prices even a pauper could afford."

Today, still family owned and operated, Peter Pauper Press continues to honor our founders' legacy—and our customers' expectations—of beauty, quality, and value.

Designed by David Cole Wheeler
Illustrations used under license from Shutterstock.com
Copyright © 2021
Peter Pauper Press, Inc.
202 Mamaroneck Avenue
White Plains NY 10601
All rights reserved
ISBN 978-1-4413-3704-7
Printed in China
7 6 5 4 3 2 1
Visit us at www.peterpauper.com

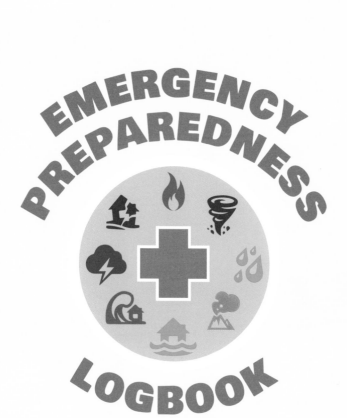

EMERGENCY PREPAREDNESS

LOGBOOK

CONTENTS

INTRODUCTION

The word "emergency" is defined as "an unforeseen combination of circumstances or the resulting state that calls for immediate action."*

Whether a natural disaster, be it a tornado, hurricane, winter storm, or a human act of terrorism, an emergency often happens without warning, is likely dangerous, and demands quick action. An emergency may occur when you or other family members are away from home, compounding a crisis. And it's true: Emergency and disaster events are happening more often around the world.

But there are practical, common-sense things we can do to be prepared and protect our families. Among the most important things:

☐ **Create an emergency plan, including a communications plan and an evacuation plan.**

☐ **Collect and secure essential supplies that may be needed in case of emergency.**

This logbook offers ideas for both, starting on page 107.

It also offers checklists that pertain to specific disasters, to jump-start your response to and recovery from an emergency situation.

Throughout, we've supplied plenty of Notes pages in which you can record your thoughts, plans, ideas, and vital information that pertains specifically to you and your family.

We can't prevent emergencies from happening. But by being prepared, we gain some sense of control and peace of mind.

*Merriam-Webster.com Dictionary, s.v. "emergency," accessed November 13, 2020, https://www. merriam-webster.com/dictionary/emergency.

PLANNING FOR EMERGENCIES

An emergency can happen anytime and anywhere. Read through this log-book to learn about specific types of emergencies and disasters and what might be needed to respond to each.

Keep in mind that many emergencies result in loss of electricity, heat, and air conditioning, sometimes for days.

Use the logbook to make preparedness plans with your family. Think about what to do at home, at school, and at work.

Prepare so that you will be able to be on your own without power or phones for at least 7 to 10 days.

Consider starting with a few basic steps:

- ☐ **Start building an emergency backpack for each family member. See page 109.**

- ☐ **Compile a list of emergency contacts and post it in a prominent place in your home.**

- ☐ **Take a first aid course with your family.**

- ☐ **Get in the habit of keeping your vehicle serviced and fuel tank topped off.**

- ☐ **Do you spend a lot of time in your vehicle? Create a separate emergency kit to keep in your trunk.**

- ☐ **Think about the kinds of emergencies that are most likely to happen or have happened in your area. Power outages, flooding, severe weather? Prepare for those types of situations now, before you must go through them again.**

DISASTER CHECKLISTS

DROUGHT

A **drought** is an extended period of abnormally low precipitation. Such a period may lead to water-use restrictions in your community, such as constraints on watering lawns or washing cars.

Prepare for a drought by making it a habit to conserve water. **Bonus:** You'll save on municipal water bills.

DROUGHT

COMMON-SENSE TIPS FOR CONSERVING WATER:

☐ Plant native drought-tolerant ground covers, shrubs, and trees.

☐ Collect rainwater in barrels or containers for your garden. Rainwater is also better for plants.

☐ Raise your lawn mower blade. A higher cut encourages grass roots to grow more deeply and holds soil moisture.

☐ Mulch plants, shrubs, and trees. Mulch helps soil stay moist and helps control weeds that compete with your plants for water.

☐ Cover pools and spas to reduce water evaporation.

☐ Use extra water from cooking to water indoor or outdoor plants.

☐ Use leftover unsalted water from steamed or boiled vegetables or hard-boiled eggs to water plants. This also provides them with a nutrient boost.

☐ Fix dripping faucets. One drip every other second wastes more than 1,000 gallons (3,785 liters) of water a year.

☐ Install faucet aerators with flow restrictors.

☐ Insulate water pipes to reduce heat loss and prevent pipes from bursting in the winter.

☐ Replacing an old toilet? Consider a low-volume one that uses less than half the water.

STORE EXTRA WATER FOR EMERGENCIES:

☐ Store 1 gallon (3.78 liters) of water, per person, per day for emergencies.

☐ Store water for pets as well.

☐ Keep several jugs of water in your freezer. Use them to keep foods cold during an emergency.

☐ Make a habit of storing large and small containers of water for drinking and for emergencies.

☐ Store water in cool, dark spaces to avoid plastic degradation.

☐ Larger containers of water are handy for bathing, cleaning, and flushing toilets.

☐ Fill the bathtub with water to use for bathing, cleaning, or flushing the toilet.

DURING A DROUGHT:

☐ Follow community water restriction advisories.

☐ Take short showers. Turn on the water only to get wet and lather up, and then again to rinse.

☐ Put a pail or bucket in the shower to catch water as you wait for it to heat up. Use it to keep your plants watered.

☐ Don't let water run while brushing your teeth.

☐ Avoid flushing toilets unnecessarily.

☐ Use dishwashers only when fully loaded.

☐ Clean vegetables in a pot filled with water rather than running water from the tap.

☐ Store pitchers of drinking water in the refrigerator, instead of letting water run while you wait for it to cool.

☐ Water lawns only when needed. If the soil feels moist, or if your grass springs back when you step on it, it doesn't need watering yet.

☐ If your lawn does require watering, do so early in the morning when temperatures are cooler. Less water will evaporate.

☐ Don't leave sprinklers or hoses unattended. An average garden hose can discharge between 9 and 17 gallons (34 and 64.35 liters) of water per minute and hundreds of gallons and liters of water in an hour.

☐ Use a broom instead of your garden hose to remove leaves from your driveway or sidewalk.

NOTES:

NOTES:

NOTES:

NOTES:

NOTES:

EARTHQUAKE

An **earthquake** is a sudden, violent shaking of the ground caused by **seismic waves** within the earth's crust.

These waves of energy occur when friction causes masses of rock under stress to slip. Earthquakes can happen anywhere without warning and can also cause landslides, avalanches, fires, and floods.

The **Richter Magnitude Scale** indicates the amount of energy released, in values ranging between 1 and 9. Each increase of 1 unit represents a 32-fold increase in released energy.

An **epicenter** is the location on the earth's surface directly above the place of origin of an earthquake.

Earthquake **aftershocks** are follow-up earthquakes that occur days, weeks, or even months after an initial earthquake.

EARTHQUAKE

BEFORE AN EARTHQUAKE HAPPENS:

☐ If you live in an area that is prone to earthquakes, survey your home and identify items that might fall and injure family members, such as bookcases, shelving units, cabinets, lamps, wall-mounted mirrors, large works of art, large-screen televisions, computers, and even appliances such as refrigerators. Secure as many as possible.

☐ Identify breakable items and move them to lower shelves, or store them in closed cabinets with sturdy latches.

☐ Store flammable household items on bottom shelves in closed, latched cabinets.

☐ Engage a home inspector or building engineer to advise on improvements you can make to ensure your home is more earthquake-resilient.

☐ Check with your insurance agent about obtaining earthquake coverage.

☐ Before an earthquake, practice **Drop** (sometimes called "Lock"), **Cover**, and **Hold On** with family members:

☐ **Drop**. Wherever you are, if things start shaking, drop to your hands and knees and hold onto something sturdy. If you use a wheelchair or walker with a seat, lock your wheels and stay seated until the shaking stops. If you are unable to drop, bend forward, cover your head with your arms, and hold onto your neck with both hands.

☐ **Cover**. Cover your head and neck with your arms. Crawl underneath something sturdy, such as a desk or table. If you cannot, then crawl to an interior wall away from windows. Do not crawl through falling or fallen debris. Stay on your knees or stay bent over to protect internal organs.

☐ **Hold On**. If you are under a desk or table, hold on with one hand and be ready to move with it.

DURING AN EARTHQUAKE:

☐ Stay inside. If you venture out, especially in urban areas, you may be hit by falling debris, such as brick, glass, and metal.

☐ If inside your home, workplace, or other location: Move to an interior room away from windows, outside walls, skylights, mirrors, and furnishings that could fall. Avoid doorways.

☐ Do not run for an exit. Do not use an elevator. Drop, get under, and hold onto a sturdy piece of furniture. Stay on the same floor.

☐ If you are in a moving vehicle, and if it is possible, drive away from buildings, utility wires, trees, and overpasses. Stop the vehicle. Apply the parking brake.

AFTER AN EARTHQUAKE:

☐ Beware of aftershocks. These can be as strong or stronger than the initial earthquake. Be ready to **Drop**, **Cover**, and **Hold On**.

☐ If you are inside a damaged structure, get outside as quickly as you can. But beware of falling objects, downed utility lines, hung-up tree limbs that could fall, etc.

☐ If you are trapped inside, text for help, or bang on a wall or door. Carry a whistle with you and use it instead of shouting for help.

☐ Cover your eyes, nose, and mouth if dangerous dust and debris particles are filling the air.

☐ If you are in an area where tsunamis could occur (see page 81), move inland or to higher ground when the shaking stops.

☐ Monitor local news reports, alerts, and notifications.

☐ Follow safety protocols when cleaning up.

☐ Phone systems become busy during emergencies. Send text messages or use social media to communicate with loved ones.

NOTES:

NOTES:

NOTES:

NOTES:

NOTES:

FIRE SAFETY

FIRE SAFETY

PRACTICE COMMON-SENSE FIRE SAFETY:

☐ Remove fire hazards around your home: fallen branches, leaves, and miscellaneous flammable objects, materials, or debris.

☐ Remove fire hazards within the home. De-clutter combustible stacks of papers, magazines, etc.

☐ Store flammable household items (nail polish remover, paint thinner, aerosol cans, etc.) carefully.

☐ Make sure smoke detectors function and have fresh batteries. Install detectors on every level of your home and in every bedroom. Test them once a month. Clean and inspect them and replace batteries twice a year (remember by simply replacing them when Daylight Saving Time occurs).

☐ Obtain a fire extinguisher and make sure family members know how to operate it.

☐ Have your chimney and fireplace inspected each year.

☐ Pay attention when cooking. Wear short sleeves or tight sleeves. Keep paper towels, kitchen towels, and oven mitts away from burners.

☐ Do not use candles or smoke indoors.

☐ Use fire-resistant materials when repairing or renovating your home.

☐ Keep important documents in a fireproof safe.

☐ Inspect extension, appliance, and other cords periodically for damage.

☐ Keep in mind: Home fires outnumber other building fires by more than 3 to 1, generally because public buildings have mandatory safety requirements. Homes do not. For your family's sake, fireproof your home.

Note:

Wool is an incredible natural flame-resistant fiber, and is often used in the manufacture of essential workers' Personal Protective Equipment (PPE) for that reason. The use of wool clothing, carpets, bedding, and soft furnishings provides your family and home with extra levels of protection from fire.

IN CASE OF A KITCHEN FIRE:

☐ Extinguish cooking fires with baking soda. Do not use water or flour. Flour is flammable.

☐ Smother oven or broiler fires by keeping the oven door closed. Turn off the oven.

- [ ] Smother cooktop oil and grease fires by sliding a pan lid over the flames. Turn off the burner. Do not attempt to carry the pan outside. Wait for the pan to cool.
- [ ] Make a fire safety plan:
- [ ] Use the grid-patterned pages on 24 and 25 to draw a floor plan of your home. Draw each floor and note the locations of doors, windows, and stairs. Draw at least 2 escape routes from each room with different colored pencils or markers. Note the locations of fire extinguishers, first aid kits, and emergency kits.
- [ ] Meet with your family and decide which exits each family member will use in the event of a fire.
- [ ] Have a plan for daytime, weekends, and during the night. (Most fatal fires occur between midnight and 8 a.m., when people are sleeping.)
- [ ] Determine a family meeting place outside in your neighborhood in case of a house fire.
- [ ] Rehearse your plan and time how long it takes each member to exit the house and get to the predetermined meeting place.

DURING A FIRE:

- [ ] If your smoke detector goes off, or you smell smoke, leave NOW. (Toxic gases and extreme heat can travel faster than flames. You may have less than 2-1/2 minutes to leave!)
- [ ] Call the fire department immediately.
- [ ] Before leaving the room you are in, feel the door with the back of your hand. If it is hot or warm, do not open it.
- [ ] If the door is not warm, open it and check outside. If you see smoke, shut the door. If you do not see smoke, leave the house or building immediately.
- [ ] Do not use a building elevator during a fire. Take the stairs.
- [ ] Once outside, go to your family meeting place. Do not return to your house.

IF YOU CANNOT LEAVE:

- [ ] If at all possible, place wet, rolled-up towels at the base of each door or seal doors with duct tape. Seal any other openings, such as vents.
- [ ] Go to a window in your room. If there is a fire below, keep the window closed, but stay near the window to wave for help. If there is no fire, open the window and hang a scarf, towel, pillowcase, etc., from it to let people know you need help and locate where you are.
- [ ] Wait for rescue. Stay calm.

NOTES:

Use these pages to draw a floor plan of your home. Draw each floor and note the locations of doors, windows, and stairs. Use different colored pencils or markers to draw at least 2 escape routes from each room in the event of a fire or other emergency.

NOTES:

FLOOD

Flooding, the rise and overflow of large quantities of water onto a normally dry area, is one of the most frequently occurring natural disaster events in the world. A flood can result from sudden torrential rains, hurricanes, snow melt, or damage to man-made water systems, such as dams.

A **flood watch** or **flash flood watch** means there is potential for flooding after significant rainfall, or perhaps after a dam or levee failure, etc.

A **flood warning** or **flash flood warning** cautions that flooding, of rivers and streams, or in a normally dry area, is impending. **Take action!**

FLOOD

BEFORE A FLOOD:

☐ Determine if you are in a flood-prone area. Find out how high your home is above (or below) possible flood levels. FEMA provides resources related to flood mapping, flood insurance, etc.: **www.fema.gov**.

☐ If your basement is prone to flooding, install a sump pump with back-up power.

☐ Have a licensed electrician raise electric components (switches, sockets, circuit breakers, and wiring) at least 1 foot (30.48 centimeters) above your home's projected flood elevation.

☐ Install backflow valves or plugs to prevent floodwaters from entering drains, toilets, etc.

☐ Anchor basement fuel tanks.

☐ Stock up and use flood-related supplies, such as sheets of plywood and sandbags.

☐ Move furniture and household items to upper floors.

☐ Secure items you have outside, such as patio furniture, trash cans, etc.

☐ Be prepared to evacuate. Determine the best route to take from your home to higher, safer ground. Review family emergency and evacuation plans (see section beginning with page 107).

☐ Add rubber boots, waterproof gloves, and mosquito/insect repellent to your emergency kit. Pack long-sleeved shirts and pants for the family to protect from mosquitoes which breed in standing flood waters.

☐ Be prepared to turn off the electric, gas, and water. Unplug appliances.

☐ Close and lock windows and doors.

DURING A FLOOD:

☐ If you must evacuate, leave as soon as you can to avoid becoming trapped on crowded or flooded roadways.

☐ Monitor news reports for updated information.

☐ Beware of washed-out roads, bridges, downed power lines, fallen trees, etc.

☐ Beware of streams and rivers that may suddenly rise.

☐ Do not drive on flooded roads. Water moving at 2 miles per hour (3.22 kilometers per hour) can sweep a car off a road or bridge. Most flash flood deaths occur in automobiles.

☐ If you are trapped in your vehicle in flood waters, stay inside. If water begins rising within the vehicle, get on the roof.

- [ ] Do not walk or swim in flood waters, which may be contaminated and contain hazardous debris. Underground or downed lines can also electrically charge waters.

- [ ] If flood waters are rising in your home, move to an upper floor. Don't go into a closed attic; you may be trapped inside by flood waters.

AFTER A FLOOD:

- [ ] Only return home when there is an official "all-clear."

- [ ] If your home has been flooded, be aware that there may be wild animals, reptiles, and other creatures inside. Wear protective clothing, gloves, and work boots.

- [ ] Beware of the danger of electrocution. Stay away from downed power lines.

- [ ] Use generators properly—never inside your home.

- [ ] Take stock of damage and contact your insurance company. Document damage with photos.

- [ ] Phone systems become busy during emergencies. Send text messages or use social media to communicate with loved ones.

NOTES:

NOTES:

NOTES:

NOTES:

NOTES:

HEAT WAVE

An official **heat wave** is defined as more than 48 hours of 90-degree Fahrenheit (32.2 degrees Celsius) heat and 80% relative humidity or higher.

Relative humidity is how much water vapor is in the air, compared to how much the air could hold. For example, a relative humidity of 50% means the air is holding half of the water vapor it could hold.

Heat index is determined by adding the relative humidity to the actual temperature. This indicates how hot it feels to us.

Extreme heat can cause a variety of conditions, with **heat stroke** or **sunstroke** the most serious. If one's body temperature gets too hot, heat stroke can cause brain injury or death! Symptoms include: loss of consciousness, shallow breathing, hot, red skin, and a rapid pulse. Get medical help now. Try to lower body temperature immediately with a cool bath or cool cloths.

Heat exhaustion occurs when people over-exert themselves outdoors in hot, humid weather, whether working outdoors or participating in sports. If you are sweating profusely, feel dizzy and nauseous, or feel like passing out, get out of the sun and into a cooler place. Drink water. If you start throwing up, feel worse, or if symptoms last more than an hour, get medical help.

Heat cramps result in muscle spasms in the legs and/or abdominal pain. This may be due to a loss of water and salt after heavy sweating. Stop, cool off, and drink water or a sports drink. If symptoms continue or if you are on a low-sodium diet or have a heart condition, get medical help.

A **heat rash** is evidenced by a rash or cluster of small blisters resembling blemishes on the skin. Get out of the sun. Keep the rash dry with baby powder or cornstarch.

Sunburns can result in painful skin, redness, blistering, fever, and headaches. Get out of the sun and into a cool bath or use cool cloths on sunburned areas. Get medical help if symptoms are severe.

You'll find more information on these terms at **www.cdc.gov/disasters/extremeheat/warning.html**.

HEAT WAVE

BEFORE A HEAT WAVE:

☐ Keep in mind that those most affected by a heat wave tend to be the elderly, small children, overweight individuals, those with alcohol issues, and those taking certain medications.

☐ Make use of weather stripping, attic fans, and other home improvement methods to keep your home cooler.

☐ Or locate places in your community with air conditioning—libraries, shopping centers, theaters, and/or local cooling centers, if needed.

DURING A HEAT WAVE:

☐ Avoid strenuous outdoor activities, especially between 11:00 a.m. and 4:00 p.m.

☐ Get your daily walk or jog out of the way early in the morning, optimally by 7:00 a.m.

☐ During the day, stay out of the sun and in an air-conditioned space, if possible.

☐ Keep curtains or drapes closed to help keep heat out.

☐ Drink plenty of fluids, but avoid caffeine and alcohol.

☐ Eat small meals more frequently. But eat light. Eat more fruits and vegetables. Protein causes water loss as it increases metabolic heat.

☐ Make sure pets have fresh water. Keep them inside.

☐ If you must go out, use sunscreen. Wear a hat and loose, lighter-colored clothing.

☐ Check on neighbors.

☐ Do not leave people or pets in parked vehicles in the heat. Temperatures can quickly reach 140 degrees Fahrenheit (60 degrees Celsius), which can kill in minutes.

☐ Conserve energy and help prevent power outages! Set your AC to 78 degrees Fahrenheit (26 degrees Celsius), no lower, and use it only when you are home. Use supplementary fans to help distribute the cooler air.

☐ Operate washers, dryers, and other major appliances early in the morning or late at night.

NOTES:

NOTES:

NOTES:

HURRICANE

Hurricanes are occurring in record numbers. These tropical storms cause damage with high winds, torrential rains, and storm surges, not just along coastal areas, but inland as well.

A **hurricane watch** indicates that a hurricane may threaten your area within the next 48 hours.

A **hurricane warning** means that hurricane conditions—winds of 74 miles per hour (119 kilometers per hour) or more and high tides and waves—are expected within the next 36 hours. **Get ready now.**

A **flash flood watch** means there is potential for flash flooding.

A **flash flood warning** means flash flooding is imminent in your area. **Beware!**

HURRICANE

BEFORE A HURRICANE:

☐ Monitor national, regional, and local news alerts and notifications for updates on approaching storms.

☐ Review your emergency plan and emergency kits. Procure any supplies you need. See pages 109–111. You may not be able to obtain them for days and weeks after a hurricane.

☐ Prepare your property: Secure patio furniture, trash cans, and other loose items. Clean gutters and drains. Obtain plywood and use it to secure structures.

☐ Moor your boat or store it securely.

☐ See page 55 for what to do if you anticipate power outages.

DURING A HURRICANE:

☐ Be prepared to evacuate. Review your evacuation plan and routes. See page 118.

☐ Shelter in an interior room during high winds.

☐ If your building is flooded, go to the highest floor. But do not enter a closed attic as you may become trapped.

☐ Do not drive, walk, or swim through flood waters. Just 1 foot (30.48 centimeters) of moving flood water can take your vehicle away. Six inches (15.24 centimeters) can knock you down and sweep you away.

AFTER A HURRICANE:

☐ Monitor post-hurricane news and announcements. Do not return home until there is an official "all-clear."

☐ Abide by proper protocols when cleaning up after a hurricane. Wear protective masks, clothing, heavy gloves, and sturdy, rubber-soled shoes.

☐ Inspect your property for damage. Document damage with photos. Contact your insurance company.

☐ Do not go near downed lines. Report these to local police and utility companies.

☐ Do not touch electrical equipment during flooding or rain.

☐ Look above you for broken tree limbs caught up in lines or in tree branches—these could fall at any time.

☐ Do not wade in flood waters without proper boots or footwear—the water could hide hazardous debris, conduct electricity, or contain infectious organisms.

☐ Phone systems remain busy after emergencies. Send text messages or use social media to communicate with loved ones.

NOTES:

NOTES:

NOTES:

NOTES:

LANDSLIDE

Landslides occur when masses of earth, rocks, mud, and debris plunge down a slope in a **slurry** (a mix of liquids and solids).

They can be triggered by earthquakes, volcanic eruptions, wildfires, torrential rainfalls, water runoff, and snowmelt.

Landslides can move at avalanche speeds, travel far, and take up trees, large rocks, and even cars on their way, thus increasing in size.

LANDSLIDE

BEFORE A LANDSLIDE:

☐ Consider your property: Is your home on the edge of a hill or slope or in the path of drainage from above?

☐ Have you observed excess run-off during storms; new cracks in your foundation, driveway, or road; inclining or bulging walkways or retaining walls; trees leaning?

☐ If any of these conditions exist, a professional geotechnical consultant can evaluate your home and advise on remediation.

☐ If your home is in the path of a landslide or mud flow, you might consider creating a drainage channel or retaining walls, or installing concrete barriers (called k-rails). Don't divert drainage onto a neighbor's property, however. You may be liable for damage.

☐ Speak with your insurance agent if you are concerned that you are at risk of a landslide.

☐ If you believe you might be at risk, monitor news and weather reports before storms hit.

☐ During a storm, be aware of your surroundings and listen for loud, unexpected sounds, such as rumbling in the distance, running water, or tree limbs cracking.

DURING A LANDSLIDE:

☐ During a storm that might cause a landslide, monitor local news reports, alerts, and notifications, day and night. Landslide-related deaths often occur while people are sleeping.

☐ Be prepared to evacuate.

☐ Follow the instructions of local authorities.

☐ If you are outside, never try to cross flowing mud or water. Avoid low-lying areas. Move to higher ground.

☐ If you are near a stream, be aware of changes in water volume or opacity. Rising, muddy water can precede a landslide.

AFTER A LANDSLIDE:

☐ Monitor local news reports for the latest information, especially reports of flooding.

☐ Phone systems become busy during emergencies. Send text messages or use social media to communicate with loved ones.

☐ Keep away from a landslide area.

☐ If you observe damage to roads and power lines, report these to authorities.

☐ Contact your insurance company if there is damage to your home. Document damage with photographs.

☐ As soon as you can, use ground cover plantings to repair exposed ground to prevent further landslides or flooding.

NOTES:

NOTES:

NOTES:

NOTES:

NOTES:

PANDEMIC

A **pandemic** occurs when the outbreak of a disease affects multiple countries. Viruses, which spread easily, are the main cause of pandemics. It may take months or years for pandemic tests, treatments, and vaccines to be developed and become widely available to the public.

Coronavirus Disease 2019 (COVID-19) is a **novel** (new) virus. Such viruses are unforeseeable. They can spread directly from person to person, or indirectly, via contact with inanimate objects and surfaces. A person who has the virus but shows no symptoms (is **asymptomatic**) can also spread the disease.

Experts say we can expect more pandemics in the future.

PANDEMIC

BEFORE A PANDEMIC:

☐ Follow government guidelines.

☐ Stock up on necessities should you need to stay at home for an extended period:

    ☐ Medications/prescriptions.

    ☐ Toiletries: soap, shampoo, feminine supplies, etc.

    ☐ Cleaning supplies.

    ☐ Paper towels.

    ☐ Toilet paper.

    ☐ Non-perishable foods (see page 111).

    ☐ Pet supplies.

☐ Plan and prepare for remote work and school possibilities.

☐ Prepare to change short- and long-term travel, vacations, and other plans.

DURING A PANDEMIC:

☐ Wash your hands for at least 20 seconds, or use a quality hand sanitizer. (Note: Hand sanitizers with high levels of ethanol or hydroxypropyl are flammable.)

☐ Avoid touching your eyes, nose, and mouth.

☐ Stay at least 6 feet (2 meters) away from others who are not part of your household.

☐ Avoid large gatherings.

☐ Avoid small gatherings with those outside your immediate family.

☐ Cover coughs and sneezes. Sneeze into your elbow.

☐ Keep household and work surfaces clean and disinfected.

☐ Stay at home as much as is possible to limit possible spread of the disease.

☐ Cover your nose and mouth with a mask when in public.

☐ Talk to health care providers for straightforward information regarding the disease in relation to you and your family's health. Is telemedicine available?

☐ If you think you've been exposed to the disease, call your doctor and follow her or his directions.

☐ If you have a medical emergency, call now and wait for help to arrive. Wear a mask.

AS A PANDEMIC ABATES:

☐ Continue to follow guidelines and the advice of your family's health care providers.

☐ Follow protocols regarding re-opening of your workplace, businesses, schools, houses of worship, etc.

☐ Review and update your family emergency plan so you will be more prepared for the next pandemic.

NOTES:

NOTES:

NOTES:

NOTES:

NOTES:

POWER OUTAGE

A **power outage**, **blackout**, or **powercut** can happen anytime and be caused by many situations: lightning, ice storms, when trees are down, or when there is more demand than a power grid can handle.

POWER OUTAGE

BEFORE IT HAPPENS:

☐ Have your utility's customer service phone number and your account number handy to report an outage.

☐ Charge your devices.

☐ Back up computer files.

☐ Fuel your vehicles in case gas pumps are unable to function.

☐ Do you use an electric garage door opener? Locate the instructions and learn how to open and shut it manually.

☐ Get cash in advance in case you must shop and ATMs and cash registers are unable to function.

☐ Obtain bottled water for your family and pets.

☐ Fill the bathtub with water to use for drinking, washing, or flushing the toilet. If it is winter, and you are having trouble with your water supply or water pressure, you can also gather ice or snow to use for flushing the toilet.

☐ Gather battery- or crank-powered lanterns and flashlights. Keep one with you so you won't trip on things if it is dark when the power goes out.

☐ Invest in a battery- or crank-powered radio to follow local news.

☐ Obtain extra batteries.

☐ Get caught up on laundry so you will have changes of clothes.

☐ If it is cold out, gather outerwear and blankets to help family members stay warm.

☐ Cook the next meal in advance using things in the fridge/freezer that would spoil in an outage.

☐ Invest in a grill or camp stove to cook meals outdoors, if need be.

☐ Do you have a non-electric can opener on hand?

☐ Freeze containers of water; place them in your fridge or keep in the freezer to help keep food cold.

☐ If you refrigerate medicines, check with your health care provider on how long they can be kept in a closed refrigerator without power.

☐ Run the dishwasher if it's full.

☐ Consider purchasing a generator; if you do, follow directions for using it safely. Do NOT use indoors—fumes are deadly.

DURING THE OUTAGE:

- ☐ Contact your power company to let them know about the outage.
- ☐ Check on neighbors.
- ☐ If you go outside, avoid ALL downed power lines—they may be live.
- ☐ Beware of broken tree limbs that may be hung up above you in trees or power lines; they could fall at any time.
- ☐ Use your flashlights and battery-powered lanterns. Don't use candles—they may cause a fire.
- ☐ Turn off appliances to prevent them from being damaged by power surges once the power comes on again.
- ☐ Keep the fridge and freezer closed as long as you can.
- ☐ Keep one light switched "on" so you know when power is restored.
- ☐ Is it cold? Dress in layers and stay inside.
- ☐ Is it hot? Wear light clothing and stay hydrated.
- ☐ Have fresh water on hand for pets.
- ☐ Are you at work or in a multi-story building? The elevators may not work. Take the stairs.
- ☐ Trapped in an elevator? Be patient and wait for assistance. Do not attempt to force the doors.
- ☐ Limit travel as traffic lights will likely not function, resulting in distracted drivers and hazardous conditions.
- ☐ Phone systems become busy during emergencies. Send text messages or use social media to communicate with loved ones.

NOTES:

NOTES:

NOTES:

NOTES:

NOTES:

SINKHOLE

Sinkholes are depressions in the ground that may occur over time, or suddenly and rapidly.

Sinkholes may be funnel- or basin-shaped. They may have steep, vertical sides.

Sinkholes may result from **natural occurrences**, such as the collapse of an underground cave, or they may be the **result of human activity**, such as construction, mining, and drilling.

They often occur in regions where the geology includes **water-soluble bedrock**, such as limestone or gypsum, that deteriorates with time and moisture.

SINKHOLE

IDENTIFYING A POSSIBLE SINKHOLE:

☐ Be aware of sinkhole clues in your home: slanted, uneven floors, "ghost doors" that swing open or shut by themselves. These may indicate subsidence, or sinking.

☐ Outside, you may notice cracks in your patio or home foundation, water or loose dirt flowing into a depression or hole, trees leaning toward a depression in the earth, or an opening in the ground.

IF A SINKHOLE EXISTS:

☐ Stay away! The sinkhole may expand without notice.

☐ Keep children and pets away!

☐ Be prepared to leave your home. Follow your emergency plan.

☐ Contact your utility provider or local department of public works if you believe the sinkhole might damage electric, gas, water, or sewer lines.

☐ Contact your homeowners' insurance agent to find out if you are covered for damage caused by a sinkhole.

☐ Contact local and state authorities to find out about having a geologist or geo-technical engineer visit the site to determine why the sinkhole is occurring, what its possible impacts might be, and to advise on ways to mitigate the situation.

NOTES:

_____

_____

_____

_____

_____

_____

_____

_____

_____

NOTES:

NOTES:

NOTES:

TERRORISM

Terrorists and terrorist organizations use violence to menace and frighten the public and undermine authority.

Terrorists may target people, property, and infrastructure with threats, kidnappings, hijacking, explosives, biological and chemical agents, cyber-attacks, and other means to get their message across and gain media coverage for their causes.

The United States Federal Emergency Management Agency offers detailed information on recognizing and responding to specific terrorist acts, such as explosions, biological attacks, chemical attacks, and more, at **www.fema.gov/pdf/ areyouready/terrorism.pdf**.

TERRORISM

PREVENT TERRORISM:

☐ First, as for any emergency or disaster, be prepared to live for several days without power, phones, the Internet, ATMs, cash registers, and so on. Have family emergency plans and emergency kits in place. (See section beginning on page 107.)

☐ Simply be alert and aware of your surroundings as you go about your day.

☐ Observe daily patterns where you live, work, or go to school.

☐ Take note if you get a gut feeling that something is not right. For example, you may observe someone asking for information about a company's operations, taking photos surreptitiously, or walking into a secure area as if to test for security system vulnerabilities.

☐ Note the location of emergency exits wherever you go.

☐ Note packages, bags, devices, and objects that don't look right, seem out of place, or are abandoned. Report them.

☐ Beware when traveling. Never leave luggage unattended.

☐ Be aware of conversations in eateries, at gatherings, or on a train, plane, etc. If you overhear talk about belonging to terrorist organizations or planning attacks, pay attention.

☐ If you feel you've observed something suspicious, do NOT take action yourself. Do NOT confront anyone. Do NOT reveal how you feel. Instead, DO note details and DO report your suspicions to authorities ASAP.

☐ Keep in mind: Who did you see? What did you see? Where did you see it? When did you see it? Why did you think it was suspect?

BEFORE THE NEXT POSSIBLE TERRORIST ATTACK:

☐ Have your family emergency plans in place and make sure everyone knows how to follow them and what to do. See section beginning on page 107. Review your plans with your family once a month.

DURING A TERRORIST EVENT:

☐ Stay calm.

☐ Monitor news reports, alerts, and notifications for the latest information.

☐ Follow the instructions of emergency officials.

☐ If you happen to be in the vicinity of the event, call authorities. Check for injuries. Assist others.

- [ ] In an explosion, try to get under a sturdy desk, table, or counter, as you would in an earthquake (page 15).

- [ ] After an explosion, leave the building you're in immediately. Use the stairs.

- [ ] Use your phone's flashlight if your building or home is dark. Do not turn on electrical switches.

- [ ] Once outside, stay away from glass and windows which could further explode. Watch for falling debris.

- [ ] If you are trapped, don't call out. Cover your mouth and nose so as not to inhale hazardous dust particles and debris. Call attention to your location by using your phone's flashlight, by using a whistle, or by banging on walls, pipes, and so on.

- [ ] Follow your emergency plan. Evacuate if you are advised to do so.

- [ ] If you are advised to shelter in place, get all family members and pets inside your home.

- [ ] Close and lock doors and windows.

- [ ] Turn off the heat or AC, vents, and fans.

- [ ] Select an interior room in which the family may shelter, preferably one that is windowless and on an upper level. This is in case of a possible chemical attack. (Some chemical agents are heavier than air, though they may seep into basements and lower levels.)

- [ ] Bring your emergency kits into the room.

- [ ] Monitor news reports.

- [ ] Wait for an "all-clear" before you exit the room or your home.

- [ ] Phone systems become busy during emergencies. Send text messages or use social media to communicate with loved ones.

NOTES:

NOTES:

67

NOTES:

NOTES:

NOTES:

THUNDERSTORM

A **thunderstorm** is an electrically charged storm system that produces **lightning**, which, in turn, heats the air, producing shock waves we hear as claps of **thunder**. Thunderstorms often occur in hot, humid conditions and can produce sudden, heavy rains. Sometimes they are called **lightning storms** or **electrical storms**.

Your chances of being struck by lightning are estimated to be 1 in 600,000.

A person can be injured or killed by a **direct lightning strike**; by a **side flash**, when lightning strikes a taller object, such as a tree, and the current jumps over to a person who is close to the taller object; by a **ground current**, when the energy from a lightning strike travels outward and in and along the ground surface; by **conduction**, via paths provided by metal wires, plumbing, even windows and doors; or (infrequently) by ground-based **lightning streamers**, which are attracted to charged **lightning leaders** above, causing a strike. Learn more at **www.weather.gov/safety/lightning-struck**.

A **severe thunderstorm watch** is an alert to let you know that weather conditions close to your area **may** result in strong storms with lightning, hail, and damaging winds.

A **severe thunderstorm warning** is an alert to let you know that a strong storm with lightning, hail, and/or damaging winds will be moving through your area shortly. **Take cover. Stay inside.**

THUNDERSTORM

DURING A THUNDERSTORM:

☐ If you are outside and hear thunder, you are close enough to be hit by lightning. Seek shelter now.

☐ If you must remain outside, try to find a low spot away from trees and utility poles. If you are in a wooded area, shelter under low trees.

☐ If flash flooding is a possibility, head to higher ground.

☐ If you feel your skin tingling, or if your hair stands on end, squat low to the ground. Place your hands on your knees with your head between them. Make yourself the smallest target possible. Minimize contact with the ground.

☐ If you can, take cover in a building or in a hard-top vehicle.

☐ Do not drive if flooding is possible. Most flash flood deaths occur in automobiles.

☐ If you are in a boat, head for shore immediately. Get out of the water.

☐ Telephone lines and metal pipes can conduct electricity. Avoid using telephone landlines and appliances.

☐ Turn off air conditioners. Power surges from lightning can overload and damage compressors.

☐ Avoid taking a bath or shower during a thunderstorm. Water conducts electricity, and if lightning hits your home, there is a possibility you could be electrocuted.

☐ Follow the **30-30 Rule**: Count the seconds between seeing a flash of lightning and hearing thunder. If you hear thunder before you get to 30 seconds, lightning is a threat. Seek shelter now. Then, after you hear the last rumble of thunder, wait at least 30 minutes before leaving your shelter.

☐ **Determine how far way you are from lightning**: Count the number of seconds between the flash of lightning and the sound of thunder. Divide by 5. The result will tell you the approximate distance in miles from you to the lightning: 15 seconds = 3 miles (4.83 kilometers), 5 seconds = 1 mile (1.61 kilometers). 0 seconds = too close.

NOTES:

NOTES:

NOTES:

TORNADO

Tornadoes are rapidly whirling winds (hence the nickname "twisters") that occur during thunderstorms. They are known for their funnel-shaped columns of air that move in narrow paths over the surface of the land. They can be extremely destructive.

What is a **tornado watch**? This is an alert to let you know that weather conditions close to your area may result in severe thunderstorms and/or tornadoes.

What is a **tornado warning**? This is an alert to let you know that a tornado will be moving through your area shortly. **Take cover now**.

TORNADO

BEFORE A TORNADO:

☐ Monitor weather reports, alerts, and notifications, especially when thunderstorms are expected.

☐ Keep an eye out for a funnel-shaped cloud or a moving cloud of debris; hail; and dark, greenish skies.

☐ Listen for a sound like that of a freight train.

☐ If you are outside, seek shelter in a substantially constructed building. If this is not possible, find a ditch or low spot. Lie down flat and face down. Cover your head and neck with your hands and arms.

☐ If you are in a vehicle, leave it.

☐ If you are in a manufactured or mobile home, if at all possible, get out and get to a more substantial structure immediately.

☐ When taking cover in a building: Go to the basement or to a windowless interior room on the lowest floor of the building. Take the stairs. Do not use elevators.

☐ Get into a closet, a bathroom, or other interior space. Get under something sturdy, such as a heavy table. Climb under a mattress. Get into a bathtub and lie low. Cover yourself with a blanket.

DURING A TORNADO:

☐ If you are outside, do not get under bridges or overpasses. Move to a low, flat location, such as a dry ditch.

☐ Beware of flying and falling debris.

☐ Protect your head and neck with your arms. Cover yourself with a coat if possible.

☐ If at home, put on a helmet: football, hockey, motorcycle, or other helmet, if available.

☐ If you are inside, keep away from windows, which could explode, as well as doors and exterior walls.

☐ If you are at work, school, or in a shopping center: Stay away from windows and large open areas. Do not leave to go to your vehicle. Get under a heavy piece of furniture, such as a desk, table, or store counter.

☐ Never try to outrun a tornado in a vehicle. Get out of your car and move to a low, flat location.

AFTER A TORNADO:

- [ ] If you are trapped, first cover your mouth with a cloth or mask to avoid breathing in dangerous dust and particles. Let people know where you are by sending a text. Or bang on a wall or a pipe, or use a whistle to attract attention.
- [ ] Keep abreast of updated information.
- [ ] Do not go near downed power lines.
- [ ] Do not enter damaged structures until you have an official "all-clear" to do so.
- [ ] Take care when navigating debris and undergoing clean-up. Many tornado-related injuries, such as puncture wounds from nails, cuts from broken glass, and injuries from suspended debris that drops, falling tree limbs, etc., happen after tornadoes. There is also danger of electrocution, fire, or explosion from electric and gas lines.
- [ ] Follow proper clean-up protocols. Wear appropriate clothing: long pants, gloves, and sturdy footwear.
- [ ] Phone systems become busy during emergencies. Send text messages or use social media to communicate with loved ones.

NOTES:

NOTES:

NOTES:

NOTES:

NOTES:

TSUNAMI

A **tsunami** is an enormous ocean wave, or series of waves, caused by earthquakes, volcanic eruptions, or undersea landslides. They may move as fast as 30 miles per hour (48.28 kilometers per hour) and reach 100 feet (30.48 meters) in height.

Tsunamis are not **tidal waves**, which are large waves caused by the gravitational interactions of the sun, moon, and earth.

The United States National Oceanic and Atmospheric Administration (NOAA)/National Weather Service issues tsunami **watches**, **advisories**, and **warnings** for the U.S. and Canada, and **tsunami threats** for the international community at **www.tsunami.gov**.

TSUNAMI

IF A TSUNAMI THREATENS:

☐ Monitor news reports, alerts, and notifications.

☐ Be ready to evacuate. Review family emergency and evacuation plans.

☐ Evacuation routes may be marked by signs containing an image of a wave with an arrow pointing in the direction of higher ground.

☐ If an earthquake proceeds the tsunami, refer to earthquake procedures (page 15).

☐ Watch for signs of a tsunami, such as a loud roar from the sea, a sudden rise of ocean levels, or a draining of the ocean so that you can actually see the ocean floor.

☐ Leave before or as soon as local authorities instruct you to do so.

☐ Go as far inland as you can to the highest ground you can travel to.

☐ If you are on a boat in a harbor, get ashore as soon as possible, then head inland.

DURING A TSUNAMI:

☐ Monitor local news for the latest information.

☐ If you are in tsunami waters, try to grab something floating nearby, such as a tree limb or barrel. Hang on.

☐ If you are on the water in a boat or vessel, face the direction of the waves and head out to sea as fast as possible.

AFTER A TSUNAMI:

☐ Only return home when there is an official "all-clear."

☐ Do not wade in flood waters, which may be contaminated and contain hazardous debris. Underground or downed lines can also electrically charge waters.

☐ If your home has been flooded, be aware that there may be wild animals, reptiles, and other creatures inside. Wear protective clothing, gloves, and work boots.

☐ Beware of the danger of electrocution. Stay away from downed power lines.

☐ Use generators properly, never inside your home.

☐ Take stock of damage and contact your insurance company. Document damage with photos.

☐ Phone systems become busy during emergencies. Send text messages or use social media to communicate with loved ones.

NOTES:

NOTES:

NOTES:

VOLCANIC ERUPTION

A **volcanic eruption** occurs when pressure from gases and molten rock becomes great enough to be forced from a mountaintop "vent." Eruptions can be slow and quiet, or they can be violent.

Volcanic eruptions may produce super-hot lava flows, **lahars** (fast-moving mud or debris flows), dangerous gases, or spew rocks and ash.

They may also cause other disasters, such as fires, landslides, earthquakes, and flash flooding.

VOLCANIC ERUPTION

IF A VOLCANIC ERUPTION IS IMMINENT:

- ☐ Listen to local radio or television news reports for updated information.
- ☐ Make sure family members and pets are inside.
- ☐ Is ashfall a concern? Limit the penetration of outside air into your home. Close all doors and windows. Seal with duct tape. Seal all vents. Place damp towels beneath exterior doors. Do not run heating or cooling systems that draw in outside air.
- ☐ Be ready to evacuate. Don long-sleeved shirts and pants, wear sturdy shoes, have goggles and masks ready.
- ☐ Follow evacuation instructions.
- ☐ Pay attention to local reports of road closures due to lava.

IF YOU ARE OUTDOORS DURING AN ERUPTION:

- ☐ Seek indoor shelter immediately if possible.
- ☐ Listen to local radio or television news reports for information.
- ☐ Lava or lahars may flow down the mountain into low-lying areas and streams. Avoid these areas.
- ☐ Stay away from lava flows. As they burn vegetation, they produce methane gas, which may explode.
- ☐ Beware volcanic ashfall. Cover eyes, nose, mouth, and skin.
- ☐ Do not drive in ashfall. Visibility is reduced and ash makes roads slippery. Ashfall also damages vehicle engines as well as exteriors.

AFTER AN ERUPTION:

- ☐ Stay inside your home until officials declare it is safe to leave. Follow their instructions.
- ☐ Check your home for damage to roofs, walls, foundation, and utility lines.
- ☐ Notify your insurance company if your home is damaged. Document the damage with photographs.
- ☐ Clear home and building roofs of ash as soon as you can. Ashfall can be extremely heavy and may cause roofs to collapse. Follow proper ash removal and disposal protocols.
- ☐ When it is safe to drive again, clean windshield wipers of ash before use to avoid scratching your windshield.

☐ Do not drive on lahars; they are slippery, may not support the weight of your vehicle, and can pick up hazardous objects as they flow.

☐ Phone systems become busy during emergencies. Send text messages or use social media to communicate with loved ones.

NOTES:

NOTES:

NOTES:

NOTES:

NOTES:

WILDFIRE

Wildfires are widespread, destructive, uncontrolled fires that sweep through brush, fields, and woodland.

A **ground fire** is one burning on the ground or in the **understory**, the layer of vegetation (shrubs and smaller or young trees) below the forest canopy. A **crown fire** is one which ascends into a forest canopy from the ground. Wildfires can become **catastrophic fires**, burning millions of acres, adversely impacting and disrupting lives, wildlife, the environment, and local economies. You'll find more fire and wildfire terms at this United States National Park Service website: **www.nps.gov/olym/learn/management/upload/fire-wildfire-definitions-2.pdf**.

The United States National Weather Service **(www.weather.gov/safety/wildfire-ww)** issues three types of wildfire alerts: **Red Flag Warning: Take Action**. Take care with open flames as conditions for wildfires are ongoing and imminent. **Fire Weather Watch: Be Prepared**. Conditions for extensive wildland fires are possible, as are conditions for **Extreme Fire Behavior**, when a wildfire is likely to burn out of control.

Is your home or neighborhood located in or around a wooded, grassy, or brush-covered area? Make wildfire preparation part of your emergency and fire safety plans.

WILDFIRE

PRACTICE COMMON-SENSE FIRE SAFETY:

☐ Remove fire hazards and set up a defense zone around your home. Remove fallen branches, leaves, and miscellaneous flammable objects (such as patio furniture or stacks of firewood), materials, or debris. In a wildfire situation, these should be at least 30 feet (9.14 meters) from your home.

☐ Review fire safety plans and techniques with your family. Practice these. See page 21.

☐ Make sure smoke detectors function and have fresh batteries.

☐ N95 respirators/masks can prevent smoke inhalation and keep harmful particles out of the air you breathe. They are not meant for children, however. Visit **www.ready.gov/wildfires** for more information.

☐ In planning for fire safety, consider family members' health conditions, such as asthma, heart conditions, or pregnancy.

☐ Do not use candles or smoke indoors.

☐ When repairing or renovating your home, use fire-resistant materials.

☐ Keep important documents in a fireproof safe.

IF YOU ARE UNDER A WILDFIRE WARNING:

☐ If a wildfire is seen near your home, report it immediately. Call your local fire department or emergency services.

☐ Monitor local news reports and notifications for updated information and possible road closures.

☐ Make sure family members and pets are inside.

☐ Remove flammable curtains and move combustible furnishings away from windows.

☐ Turn off the gas. Move gas grills away from your home.

☐ Limit smoke penetration into your home. Close all doors and windows. Seal with duct tape. Seal all vents. Place damp towels beneath exterior doors. Do not run heating or cooling systems that draw in outside air. Have a portable indoor air cleaner on hand to keep one room as smoke-free as possible.

☐ Turn on all the lights in your home for extra visibility in case of smoke.

☐ Have vehicles packed and ready in case you need to evacuate. Keep vehicle windows closed.

☐ If you can: Position a ladder in front of your house. Affix lawn sprinklers to the roof. Turn on the water.

☐ If you have livestock: Turn them loose out of flammable shelters. If possible, have plans in place in advance to evacuate animals.

☐ If trapped, call 911. Report your location. Turn on lights to help responders find you.

☐ Phone systems become busy during emergencies. Send text messages or use social media to communicate with loved ones.

DURING A WILDFIRE:

☐ Stay inside your home or shelter (maybe an outbuilding or workshop), preferably one with a noncombustible roof and siding and dual-pane or tempered glass windows.

☐ The power will likely go out. Be prepared with flashlights and other supplies.

☐ Fill sinks, tubs, buckets, and jugs with cold water to use to extinguish any embers that may enter your shelter.

☐ Stay in the interior of your structure, away from windows and glass doors.

☐ Be forewarned: The roar of a wildfire is frightening, and your shelter will become very hot. Resist the urge to leave: It will be much hotter and much more dangerous outside. Stay calm.

☐ Monitor local news updates to get the latest emergency information.

IF YOU ARE IN A VEHICLE:

☐ Find a place to park away from trees, brush, and vegetation.

☐ Stay in the car. Keep doors and windows shut. Turn off the AC. Close air vents.

☐ Call 911 to let others know where you are.

☐ Turn on lights and flashers to help others locate you.

☐ Get down on the floor and cover up with clothing, coats, or blankets.

☐ Wait until the fire passes and outside temperatures have dropped before leaving your vehicle.

IF YOU ARE OUTSIDE:

☐ Cover your nose and mouth, with wet cloth if possible.

☐ Try to find a place away from trees, brush, and vegetation.

☐ Try to find a body of water, a stream or pond, and put it between you and the fire.

☐ Call 911 to let others know where you are.

☐ Get down in a ditch or low spot. Wet your clothes if you can or cover yourself with soil and mud.

☐ Stay down until the fire passes.

AFTER A WILDFIRE:

☐ Do not return home unless you get an official "all-clear."

☐ Avoid live embers or anything that appears to be charred or smoldering to prevent additional fires.

☐ Check your home for fire-related damage.

☐ Notify your insurance company if your home is damaged. Document the damage with photographs.

☐ Wear protective clothing when cleaning up: sturdy shoes or work boots, long-sleeved shirts, long pants, gloves, and masks.

NOTES:

NOTES:

NOTES:

WINTER WEATHER

A **winter weather advisory** indicates the possibility of a winter storm event (snow, sleet, freezing rain, or a combination of these) in the next 12 to 36 hours. Expect 4 inches (10.16 centimeters) or more of snow, depending on your area.

A **winter storm watch** means there is a probability (50% to 80%) of severe winter weather within 24 to 72 hours to allow people to prepare.

A **winter storm warning** indicates that severe winter weather—heavy snow, ice, sleet, or a combination of these—is imminent (80%) or occurring. Expect 7 inches (17.78 centimeters) of snow or more in the next 12 hours, depending on your area.

A **blizzard warning** indicates a blizzard event in the next 12 to 36 hours, with wind gusts equal to or greater than 35 miles per hour, and falling, blowing snow reducing visibility to less than 1/4 mile (.40 kilometer).

A **wind chill advisory** indicates temperatures could reach -15 degrees Fahrenheit (-21 degrees Celsius) or greater in the next 12 to 36 hours.

With a **wind chill warning**, expect temperatures to reach -25 degrees Fahrenheit (-31.6 degrees Celsius) or greater in the next 12 to 36 hours.

For more details on these terms, visit the United States Weather Service at **www.weather.gov/bgm/WinterTerms**.

WINTER WEATHER

BEFORE A WINTER STORM:

☐ If you own a snow blower, have it serviced. Make sure snow shovels and other equipment are in good condition and are at hand.

☐ Obtain rock salt to melt ice on walkways. Consider using a pet-friendly variety that won't harm pets' paws.

☐ Use sand or kitty litter for vehicle traction.

☐ Trim tree limbs that may come down on your house during a severe winter storm.

☐ Winterize your home. Insulate unheated spaces and exterior walls that contain plumbing.

☐ Have your heating system inspected.

☐ Schedule an oil delivery, if needed.

☐ Have your fireplace, wood stove, chimneys, and flues inspected.

☐ Have proper firewood and matches on hand.

☐ Check smoke alarms and change batteries if needed.

☐ Have a fire extinguisher on hand.

☐ Obtain a battery-powered carbon monoxide (C.O.) detector.

☐ If a power outage is a possibility, obtain emergency supplies and equipment. (See pages 55 and 109.) Remember your prescriptions. Remember supplies for pets.

☐ Have alternative heating equipment, such as portable heaters, available. Read the manufacturer's directions and warnings before use.

☐ Have cold-weather clothing and extra blankets ready.

☐ Be prepared to evacuate. (See page 118.)

DURING A WINTER STORM:

☐ Monitor news and weather reports and notifications for updates and conditions in your community.

☐ Keeps doors and window shut and locked to conserve heat.

☐ Close drapes or cover windows with blankets. Close off unused rooms. Block drafts with towels or rags.

☐ Storms can last for several days. Be conservative with fuel and supplies.

☐ Keep companion pets inside. Make sure livestock are sheltered with food and have access to an unfrozen water supply.

☐ Keep porches, steps, driveways, and walkways free of snow and ice to prevent accidents.

☐ Water expands as it freezes, causing pipes to burst. If temperatures are expected to become very cold, allow sink and tub faucets to drip continuously. Running water, even just a drip, can help keep pipes from freezing and bursting.

☐ Open kitchen and bathroom cabinets to allow warmer air to circulate around plumbing. (Remove harmful cleansers if children or pets are present.)

☐ Take care when using space heaters. Follow the manufacturer's directions. Position heaters away from drapes, curtains, and other flammable furnishings. Place cords so that family members won't trip over them, but do not place under rugs or floor mats. Do not use extension cords. Don't leave children or pets unattended when space heaters are on.

☐ Avoid carbon monoxide poisoning! Use generators safely, outside the home and away from windows. Don't attempt to heat your home with a gas oven. Use gas grills outside.

☐ Dress for warmth in layers: An inner layer that holds body heat (thermal under-wear); a middle layer that traps warm air close to you (natural fibers); and an outer, weather-resistant layer that protects against the elements (hats, scarves, ear muffs, mittens, coats, rain/snow pants, boots).

☐ Keep babies warm in one-piece garments, such as sleep sacks.

☐ If you feel too warm, especially while exerting yourself outside (shoveling snow, etc.) remove a layer, as perspiration can cause you to lose body heat. Stay dry.

☐ Avoid consuming caffeinated or alcoholic beverages, as they can contribute to dehydration and speed the harmful effects of cold on the body.

AFTER A WINTER STORM:

☐ Monitor news, weather, traffic reports, to find out about conditions in your community. Are roads blocked or icy? Avoid driving, and accidents, until conditions permit.

☐ Follow your health care provider's recommendations regarding exerting yourself in cold weather.

☐ Avoid overexertion and take breaks from the cold and go inside.

☐ Check on family, friends, and neighbors, especially the elderly.

☐ Phone systems become busy during emergencies. Send text messages or use social media to communicate with loved ones.

FROSTBITE AND HYPOTHERMIA

- **Dress properly for cold weather**. Wear warm hats, scarves, ear coverings, gloves or mittens, layers of clothing, thick socks, and weatherproof footwear to prevent serious winter health hazards.

- **Frostbite** occurs when exposed skin and underlying tissues freeze in extreme cold. Such exposure can cause permanent damage. Symptoms include red skin that then turns pale or white, and loss of feeling in fingers, toes, ears, and nose. Warm the victim slowly and seek medical help as soon as possible.

- **Hypothermia** occurs when exposure to the cold causes one's body temperature to drop dangerously low, below 95 degrees Fahrenheit (35 degrees Celsius). Symptoms include shivering (your body trying to warm itself), drowsiness, slurred speech, and clumsiness. Warm the victim slowly and seek medical help immediately.

WINTER STORM SUPPLY LIST FOR YOUR VEHICLE:

- ☐ Extra blankets and sleeping bags.
- ☐ Battery- or crank-powered flashlights and lanterns, headlamps.
- ☐ Battery- or crank-powered radio.
- ☐ Extra batteries.
- ☐ Extra gloves, mittens, socks, and hats.
- ☐ Hand and feet warmers.
- ☐ Sand or kitty litter for traction on slippery or icy roads.
- ☐ Windshield scraper and brush.
- ☐ Booster/jumper cables.
- ☐ Snow tire chains.
- ☐ Distress flares and light sticks.
- ☐ Whistle.
- ☐ Printed maps for GPS back-up.
- ☐ Brightly colored flags or cloths.
- ☐ Bottled water.
- ☐ Snacks and energy bars.
- ☐ Hand sanitizer, wipes, paper towels, plastic bags.
- ☐ Sunglasses.

WINTER STORM DRIVING TIPS:

☐ Keep vehicle windshields and windows clear—defogged and free of ice and snow.

☐ Slow down. Pay attention. Turn off your radio and phone. Crack a window to hear what is happening around you.

☐ Take care when braking if conditions are slippery.

☐ Allow more space than usual between your vehicle and the one in front of you.

☐ Snow drifts and tall piles of plowed or shoveled snow can hide sidewalks, pedestrians, children, and pets. Take care when driving in residential areas, near schools, parks, and playgrounds.

IF YOU BECOME STRANDED:

☐ Remain in your vehicle. Do not go in search of help unless that help is visible and close.

☐ Hang a brightly-colored cloth from your vehicle. Raise the hood. Use your hazard lights. Use interior lights at night.

☐ Run the engine occasionally and put the heater on. Crack downwind windows. Beware of carbon monoxide poisoning. Make sure the exhaust pipe is clear.

☐ Keep moving to keep your circulation going. Clap your hands. Move arms and legs.

☐ If there are others in the car, take turns sleeping. Stay close to each other for warmth.

NOTES:

NOTES:

NOTES:

NOTES:

NOTES:

AFTER A DISASTER

AFTER A DISASTER

GENERAL ADVICE:

☐ Let family and friends know you are safe. Phone systems become busy during emergencies. Send text messages or use social media to communicate with loved ones.

☐ Check the news or government websites for emergency orders and curfews.

☐ Do not enter emergency and evacuated areas until there is an official "all-clear."

☐ Avoid ALL downed power lines. Report downed lines, downed trees, utility poles, or gas odors to utility companies.

☐ Use caution if you must drive. Beware of flooding, road or bridge washouts, and storm debris on roads. Report these to authorities.

☐ When helping others, do not move seriously injured people unless they are in imminent danger of further harm.

FOOD AND WATER SAFETY:

☐ Check perishable items for spoilage. When in doubt, throw it out. Experts say thawed and refrigerated foods should be thrown out after 4 hours. Throw out food or medicine that have been in floodwaters.

☐ Canned food should be thrown out if the can is bulging or the can is open.

☐ Undamaged, unopened commercially canned foods that have been in a flood, etc., can be saved. Disinfect the cans in a bleach solution of 1/4 cup (237 millili-ters) plain, unscented bleach to 1 gallon (3.8 liters) of water. Remove labels first, then re-label, noting type of food and expiration.

☐ If you have a well, it should be pumped out and well water tested.

☐ Use your emergency stores of water, use water purification tablets as directed, or boil water to kill disease-causing viruses, bacteria, and parasites as directed by authorities until there is official word that water is safe.

☐ The United States Centers for Disease Control and Prevention recommends bringing water to a rolling boil for at least 1 minute (at elevations above 6,500 feet / 1,981 meters, boil for at least 3 minutes). If the water is cloudy, filter it first through clean cloth, a coffee filter, or paper towels, or let it stand until sediments settle, then draw off clean water. Store boiled water in clean, sanitized containers with tight lids.

☐ Improve the taste of boiled water by pouring it into another container. Let it stand for a few hours. Or add a pinch of salt to each quart / liter of water.

☐ For details on ways to disinfect, filter, and distill water, visit the CDC at: **www.cdc.gov/healthywater/emergency/making-water-safe.html**.

RETURNING HOME:

☐ Stay out of damaged buildings. Beware of structural damage. Roofs and floors could be compromised by storm damage. Fire-damaged structures could still be smoldering.

☐ Use a battery-powered flashlight when entering a damaged structure that is without power. A candle or flame may ignite trapped gas inside.

☐ Check building foundations, roofs, chimneys, and siding for damage.

☐ Have electric, gas, and water connections checked and turned on by a professional.

☐ Clean up flammable liquids and spilled medicines immediately. Leave the site if you smell gasoline or chemicals.

☐ Contact a disaster relief service if you need housing, food, clothing, etc., if these were destroyed.

☐ Take photos of damaged items and report these to your insurance company.

☐ Do not discard damaged items until you've conducted an inventory.

NOTES:

FAMILY PREPARATION

YOUR FAMILY PREPARATION GOALS:

☐ Have a family preparedness plan in place.

☐ Have a family communications plan.

☐ Have a disaster supply backpack assembled and ready for each family member.

☐ Have plans and supply kits ready for your pets.

☐ Have a family evacuation plan.

FAMILY EMERGENCY PLANNING:

☐ Meet with your family and talk about the possibility of various emergencies and disasters.

☐ Talk about how you can respond to each type of emergency.

☐ Know how to contact all family members at all times.

☐ Discuss what to do in case of power outages or injuries.

Designate 2 places for everyone to meet:

☐ A meeting place outside your home (say, at the corner) in case of a home emergency, such as a fire.

☐ A meeting place away from your home in case you cannot return.

☐ **Ask an out-of-town relative or friend to serve as an emergency contact** for everyone in your family should disaster occur and family members become separated. Make sure everyone has that number and has been instructed to check in with that person.

☐ **Keep a list of emergency numbers in a central spot**, such as a kitchen bulletin board or fridge. Include numbers for local police, the fire department, poison control, health care providers, school numbers, insurance agents, designated emergency contacts, etc.

☐ **Make sure your home has safety features**, such as smoke alarms, fire extinguishers, and carbon monoxide detectors. Make sure batteries are changed regularly for items needing batteries.

☐ **Consider making one room of your home a family "safe room"**—a basement room if you're concerned about tornadoes, or the attic if you're worried about flooding. Stock it with supplies and tools. The United States Federal Emergency Management Agency (FEMA) offers helpful information about safe rooms at **www.fema.gov/emergency-managers/risk-management/safe-rooms/resources**.

☐ **Make a complete inventory of everything in your home**. If disaster strikes, your insurance company will require this. Back up everything with photos. Start by taking photos of every room in your house and the possessions within each room.

NOTES:

EMERGENCY SUPPLIES CHECKLISTS

SURVIVAL BACKPACKS:

☐ Each family member should have their own customized kit in a backpack. Backpacks are easier to transport than suitcases and allow your hands to be free.

☐ Plan that you will need to survive for at least 7 to 10 days or more on your own.

☐ Stay within your budget and build your family's kits week by week.

☐ Add items that will comfort or entertain family members, such as stuffed animals, books, journals, decks of playing cards, handheld video games, etc.

☐ Check all items/replenish as needed on an annual basis.

A SUGGESTED LIST:

☐ Backpack.
☐ Gauze pads in various sizes.
☐ Ace bandages.
☐ Medical tape.
☐ Antiseptic wipes.
☐ Hygienic wipes.
☐ Band-aids.
☐ Medical gloves.
☐ Face masks and dust masks.
☐ Eye goggles.
☐ Whistle.
☐ Work gloves.
☐ Emergency blanket.
☐ Lanterns, headlamps, battery- or crank-operated flashlights.
☐ Battery- or crank-operated radio.
☐ Extra batteries.
☐ Manual can opener.
☐ Multi-tool with pliers.
☐ Reflective vest.
☐ Sleeping bag.

FOOD AND WATER:

- ☐ 7- to 10-day supply of non-perishable food (see next page).
- ☐ Canned foods.
- ☐ Non-perishable snacks: energy bars, nuts, dried fruit, etc.
- ☐ Water purification tablets.
- ☐ 7- to 10-days' worth of water (1 gallon [3.8 liters] of water per person, per day).
- ☐ Pet food.
- ☐ Water for pets.
- ☐ Eating utensils.

SUPPLIES FOR HEALTH AND HYGIENE:

- ☐ Prescriptions, medications, vitamins, supplements.
- ☐ Toilet paper.
- ☐ Wipes.
- ☐ Paper towels.
- ☐ Hand sanitizer.
- ☐ Toothbrushes, toothpaste.
- ☐ Travel-sized soaps, shampoos, deodorants, etc.
- ☐ Feminine hygiene supplies.
- ☐ Changes of clothing.

PRACTICAL SUPPLIES:

- ☐ Glow sticks.
- ☐ Duct tape.
- ☐ Scissors.
- ☐ Printed maps of the area.
- ☐ Paper, pencils, pens; journal; planner.
- ☐ Permanent markers.
- ☐ Waterproof matches.
- ☐ Solar and other cell phone chargers.
- ☐ Essential documents holder or binder.
- ☐ Plastic bags.

BASIC NON-PERISHABLE FOODS AND INGREDIENTS FOR BACKPACK AND KITCHEN:

Check expiration dates periodically, use older items first, then replenish.

- [ ] Canned meats and fish.
- [ ] Canned vegetables and fruits.
- [ ] Jarred fruits, such as applesauce.
- [ ] Canned soups.
- [ ] Dry soup mixes, ramen soups.
- [ ] Canned ravioli, chili, etc.
- [ ] Dehydrated foods, such as potato flakes.
- [ ] Freeze-dried meals and foods.
- [ ] Dried mushrooms.
- [ ] Pasta and canned or jarred sauces.
- [ ] Beans and dried bean soup mixes.
- [ ] Lentils.
- [ ] Baking ingredients and substitutes, if you are able to bake.
- [ ] Spices and herbs.
- [ ] Powdered milk.
- [ ] Juices and sports drinks.
- [ ] Dry cereals, oatmeal, grits.
- [ ] Crackers and pretzels.
- [ ] Rice, rice cakes.
- [ ] Nuts and trail mixes.
- [ ] Peanut butter.
- [ ] Dried fruit.
- [ ] Protein and energy bars.
- [ ] Food as needed for infants and toddlers.
- [ ] Bottled water.
- [ ] Coffee, tea, and cocoa.
- [ ] Comfort foods, treats, and beverages.

- [ ] In addition, before an emergency, consider stocking up on nutritious produce that is perishable but may be stored for weeks in a cool, dark, dry place, such as apples; potatoes and sweet potatoes; acorn, butternut, and other winter squashes; rutabaga, parsnips, turnips; and so on.

NOTES:

FAMILY PREPARATION

FAMILY MEMBERS WITH SPECIAL NEEDS

☐ Find out about back-up power supplies for essential medical equipment. Learn how to operate these. Keep instruction manuals at hand, or label and attach instructions to the equipment.

☐ Keep manual equipment, such as a manual wheelchair, as back-up for electric equipment.

☐ Obtain extra back-up equipment if possible, and store at your workplace or at a neighbor's.

☐ Teach those who may need to help you how they can assist.

☐ Consider purchasing a medical alert system that will allow you to call for help, should you need it.

☐ If you are physically impaired, arrange for a friend or neighbor to inform you of news related to emergencies.

☐ If you have a professional caregiver, ask their agency if they will be allowed to help you at another location, such as a shelter, should you need to evacuate.

☐ Keep your cell phone charged. Keep a list of emergency contacts and phone numbers handy.

☐ Engage at least 3 people you know and trust—family members, friends, or neighbors—to support and assist you in the case of emergency or disaster.

☐ Assess what you will need in case of an emergency. Make a record of this for caregivers. Your record may include assistance for a service animal, a shower chair, etc. Keep your record in a waterproof document holder. Make sure your caregivers know where this is.

NOTES:

NOTES:

NOTES:

CARING FOR PETS

☐ Make sure your pets are inside your home if you anticipate a storm or other emergency.

☐ Collars, tags, microchips, etc., will aid in your pets' return should they become separated.

☐ Make a list of pet-related phone numbers to call should your pet become separated: your local animal control, shelters, and emergency veterinary hospitals.

☐ Use permanent marker to write your pet's name and your name and contact information on pet carriers. Affix a photo of the pet. List any medical conditions or behavioral issues.

☐ If you MUST leave an animal behind, post a sign on your door stating "Pets Inside" and include your pet's name and your name and contact information. Affix a photo of the pet.

☐ Talk to friends, family, and neighbors about caring for your pets or theirs should an emergency arise.

☐ Make a contact list of pet-friendly hotels, motels, shelters, kennels, and veterinary hospitals outside your area should you need to evacuate.

PET SUPPLIES LIST:

☐ Extra harnesses or leashes.

☐ A long lead and yard stake for dogs.

☐ Pet carrier.

☐ Blanket to cover pet carrier.

☐ Pet toys.

☐ Litter box.

☐ Enough pet food for 7 to 10 days in an airtight container. (Change this out every 2 months.)

☐ Enough water for 7 to 10 days for each pet. (Keep in a cool, dark place and change out every 2 months.)

☐ A week's worth of litter or bedding. Note: newspaper or magazines can be used in a pinch for cat litter. Line the litter box with sections of newspaper or pages from a magazine. Then tear up paper "leaves" (large and small) and put them on top. Bonus: No messy cat litter dust or "tracking."

☐ Paper towels, cleanser, hand sanitizer, plastic bags, etc., for cleaning up after your pet.

NOTES:

YOUR EVACUATION PLAN

Part of emergency preparedness is thinking about the possibility that you may have to leave your home, and that you may have to do so with very short notice.

PLAN AHEAD:

Where you will go? (The home of a family member or friend? A hotel or motel? A shelter?)

....

....

....

Contact and other information about this location:

....

....

....

....

Alternative location in a different direction:

....

....

....

Contact and other information about this location:

....

....

....

....

Do you have pets? If so, will those locations accept pets?

ROUTES AND ALTERNATIVE ROUTES TO TAKE TO GET THERE:

☐ Save these routes on your devices. Pack printed maps for back-up.

PACK YOUR VEHICLE:

- ☐ Fuel your vehicle ASAP or make it a habit to keep it topped off—gas stations may be closed or may be unable to pump gas.

- ☐ Make it a habit to keep your vehicle serviced.

- ☐ Pack water.

- ☐ Food and snacks, can opener.

- ☐ First aid kit, medications, eyeglasses if you wear them, etc.

- ☐ Flashlights and extra batteries.

- ☐ Changes of clothes.

- ☐ Toilet paper, paper towels, wipes.

- ☐ Trash bags.

- ☐ Emergency kits/backpacks.

- ☐ Emergency documents binder.

- ☐ Paper road maps or detailed county or state atlases that show every road, with your route and alternate route highlighted in different colors.

- ☐ Devices and chargers.

- ☐ A whistle.

- ☐ A crank- or battery-powered radio and extra batteries.

- ☐ Pillows and blankets.

- ☐ Hats and gloves in the winter; bug repellent, sunscreen, hats, and rain gear in warmer seasons.

- ☐ Pets and supplies: leashes, carrier, bed, food, toys, litter box, litter.

- ☐ Wallets.

- ☐ Have cash on hand—change and large and small bills—in case registers are uable to operate.

- ☐ Ear plugs.

- ☐ Pencil, pen, and paper; a journal; a planner; books; games; activity books and crayons; etc.

SECURE YOUR HOME:

☐ Unplug TVs, computers, and appliances, and fridge and freezer if there is danger of flooding.

☐ Shut off electric, gas, and water if you are advised to do so.

☐ Close and lock windows and doors.

IF YOU MUST STAY AT A SHELTER:

☐ Keep an eye on children.

☐ Be considerate of others.

ASSIGN TASKS:

☐ Meet with family members and decide who will be in charge of what, in the event you must evacuate.

☐ Who will pack the snacks?

☐ Who will get the cat in its carrier?

☐ Who will unplug everything?

☐ Make a chart outlining who will do what and post it.

NOTES:

_____

_____

_____

_____

_____

_____

_____

_____

_____

PRACTICE YOUR PLAN AT LEAST ONCE A YEAR:

- [ ] Contact those at your destination and let them know you're doing a practice run.
- [ ] Get gas.
- [ ] Pack the car.
- [ ] Get family members and pets together.
- [ ] Grab your emergency backpack kits.
- [ ] Secure your home.
- [ ] Okay, how long did that take? How did everyone do? How can you streamline the process to an hour or less?

....

....

....

....

....

....

- [ ] Now go! Drive to your destination.
- [ ] What happened on the way? How long did it take? Adjust your plan, your destination, your route, or your supplies as needed.

....

....

....

....

....

....

NOTES:

NOTES:

124

IMPORTANT DOCUMENTS

Compile vital documents and records that would be difficult or impossible to replace, such as those listed below:

- [ ] Marriage certificate.
- [ ] Divorce records.
- [ ] Birth certificates.
- [ ] Adoption records.
- [ ] Child custody records.
- [ ] Immunization records.
- [ ] Health insurance information, medical contact information, lists of medications, allergies, etc.
- [ ] Social Security cards.
- [ ] Passports.
- [ ] Driver's licenses.
- [ ] Green card.
- [ ] Military service records.
- [ ] Pet records and tags, veterinarian information.
- [ ] Housing records: lease, mortgage, deed, insurance policy, inventory, repair services.
- [ ] Tax information: federal, state, property tax.
- [ ] Vehicles: VIN, registration, title, loan information, insurance policy.
- [ ] Other loans, automatic payments, memberships.
- [ ] Checking, savings, investments, banks.
- [ ] Pay stubs, retirement income, alimony, child support.
- [ ] Wills, trusts, power of attorney.
- [ ] Employer information.
- [ ] School information.
- [ ] Information about houses of worship.
- [ ] Business records.
- [ ] Irreplaceable personal mementos, photos, keepsakes.
- [ ] Items of value: jewelry, personal collections, works of art.
- [ ] Passwords for online accounts.

☐ Make copies of essential documents and information and keep them in a safe or fireproof and waterproof box.

☐ Extra copies can be organized and kept in a document holder or binder that you keep with you for easy reference in an emergency.

☐ Keep the binder in a secure but easily accessible location.

☐ Digital copies can be stored on a removable drive that you keep in your safe or box.

NOTES:

NOTES:

NOTES:

ESSENTIAL CONTACT INFORMATION

IMMEDIATE FAMILY MEMBERS:

Name

Contact info

Name

Contact info

Name

Contact info

Name

Contact info

Name

Contact info

Name

Contact info

Name

Contact info

Name

Contact info

Name

Contact info

LOCAL EMERGENCY CONTACTS:

Name

Address

Phone

Name

Address

Phone

Name

Address

Phone

Name

Address

Phone

Name

Address

Phone

Name

Address

Phone

Name

Address

Phone

Name

Address

Phone

Name

Address

Phone

OUT-OF-TOWN EMERGENCY CONTACTS:

Name

Address

Phone

Name

Address

Phone

Name

Address

Phone

Name

Address

Phone

Name

Address

Phone

Name

Address

Phone

Name

Address

Phone

Name

Address

Phone

Name

Address

Phone

Name

Address

Phone

NEAREST RELATIVES:

Name

Address

Phone

Name

Address

Phone

Name

Address

Phone

Name

Address

Phone

Name

Address

Phone

Name

Address

Phone

Name

Address

Phone

Name

Address

Phone

Name

Address

Phone

FAMILY WORK INFORMATION:

Name

Work Name

Work Address

Work Phone

Name

Work Name

Work Address

Work Phone

Name

Work Name

Work Address

Work Phone

Name

Work Name

Work Address

Work Phone

Name

Work Name

Work Address

Work Phone

Name

Work Name

Work Address

Work Phone

Name

Work Name

Work Address

Work Phone

SCHOOL INFORMATION:

Name

School Name

School Address

School Phone

Name

School Name

School Address

School Phone

Name

School Name

School Address

School Phone

Name

School Name

School Address

School Phone

Name

School Name

School Address

School Phone

Name

School Name

School Address

School Phone

Name

School Name

School Address

School Phone

OTHER EMERGENCY INFORMATION:

POLICE

FIRE

AMBULANCE

Hospital
Address
Phone

Doctor
Phone

Doctor
Phone

Doctor
Phone

Doctor
Phone

Doctor
Phone

Pharmacy
Address
Phone

Health Insurance
Phone

I.D. Number

Veterinarian
Address
Phone

Home Insurance

Phone

Policy Number

Auto Insurance

Phone

Policy Number

Utility Provider

Phone

Account Number

Utility Provider

Phone

Account Number

NOTES:

RESOURCES

RESOURCES

Online searches will point you to numerous websites, apps, books, and emergency prep supply sources. Here are just a few to get you started.

WEBSITES:

United States

www.ready.gov: This helpful public service website can assist you in preparing for a wide variety of emergency situations.

www.fema.gov: The Federal Emergency Management Agency strives to assist the public before, during, and after disasters.

www.cdc.gov: The Centers for Disease Control and Prevention, part of the Department of Health and Human Services, works to protect and inform the public about foreign and domestic health and safety threats.

www.noaa.gov: The National Oceanic and Atmospheric Administration monitors climate, weather, oceans, and coastlines.

www.foodsafety.gov: Offers information on recalls, outbreaks, general and emergency food safety, and more.

www.weather.gov: The National Weather Service. Enter your zip code to learn about weather outlooks, advisories, watches, warnings, and more in your area.

www.redcross.org: The Red Cross website provides preparedness tips, alerts, emergency plan templates in English and Spanish, a free Emergency App, and much more. Its store offers complete emergency kits, first aid kits, and training supplies. The Red Cross also provides a Safe and Well website at **www.redcross. org/safeandwell** which you can use to let family and friends know you are okay after a disaster.

Canada

www.publicsafety.gc.ca: Public Safety Canada deals with emergency management, along with national security, border strategies, and crime. Among its resources is a Canadian Disaster Database, providing details on over "1,000 natural, technological, and conflict events (excluding war) that have happened since 1900 at home or abroad and that have directly affected Canadians."

www.getprepared.gc.ca: An online Emergency Preparedness Guide offering helpful information in the event of many types of emergencies in Canada, plus tips for making an emergency plan and building emergency kits.

United Kingdom

www.gov.uk/government/publications/preparing-for-emergencies: The UK government offers practical strategies and publications for dealing with hazards and emergencies.

www.london.gov.uk/what-we-do/fire-and-resilience/london-resilience-partnership: London Prepared/London Resilience Partnership provides information on planning and preparing for emergencies affecting London.

https://ready.scot/: Ready Scotland strives to make its citizens resilient to emergencies.

https://gov.wales/emergency-preparation-response-recovery: The government of Wales offers information and help with emergency, preparation, response, and recovery.

www.nidirect.gov.uk/articles/emergency-situations: The government of Northern Ireland provides assistance related to emergency situations.

Australia

https://info.australia.gov.au/information-and-services/public-safety-and-law/emergency-services: The Australian government offers contact information and links for emergency and disaster assistance.

www.health.gov.au/health-topics/emergency-health-management: Australia's Department of Health provides emergency health management assistance.

International

www.worldcares.org: World Cares strives to educate, equip, and connect global citizens as Ready Responders, "able to help themselves and others when the worst happens in their community."

APPS:

www.fema.gov/about/news-multimedia/mobile-app-text-messages: The United States Federal Emergency Management Agency offers a free English/Spanish app that provides real-time National Weather Service alerts you can share via email, text, or social media, as well as safety tips, checklists, plans, and more.

www.redcross.org/get-help/how-to-prepare-for-emergencies/mobile-apps.html: The Red Cross offers several apps, including a First Aid App, a Pet First Aid App, a blood donor app, and an emergency app for those in the military and their families.

A FEW SOURCES OF SUPPLIES:

www.redcross.org: The Red Cross store offers complete emergency kits, first aid kits, training supplies, and a lot more.

www.lehmans.com: Lehman's Hardware Store carries a variety of off-the-grid merchandise and emergency supplies.

www.rainydayfoods.com: Rainy Day Foods offers everything from grains and cereals to beans, legumes, and pasta, to preparedness packs, water storage supplies, and much more.

www.beprepared.com: Be Prepared stocks bulk foods, food kits, emergency gear, offers group bulk food programs, resource links, and more.

https://buy.garmin.com/en-US/US/p/575993: Garmin is the source for highly detailed DeLorme Atlas and Gazetteer State Maps that show every road, dirt road, trail, etc., for all 50 U.S. states.

A BOOK TO GET YOU STARTED:

Prepping 101: 40 Steps You Can Take to Be Prepared: Protect Your Family, Prepare for Weather Disasters, and Be Ready and Resilient when Emergencies Arise
By Kathy Harrison
Published by Storey Publishing, North Adams, MA. 2018.
ISBN 9781612129570
$16.95 paperback

NOTES:

NOTES:

NOTES:

NOTES:

NOTES: